THE CHIC
WHO LIKED
CHOCOLATE

TERESA HEAPY

ILLUSTRATED BY
SARAH HORNE

OXFORD
UNIVERSITY PRESS

OXFORD

UNIVERSITY PRESS

Great Clarendon Street, Oxford, OX2 6DP,
United Kingdom

Oxford University Press is a department of the University of Oxford.
It furthers the University's objective of excellence in research, scholarship,
and education by publishing worldwide. Oxford is a registered trade mark of
Oxford University Press in the UK and in certain other countries

Text © Teresa Heapy 2017
Illustrations © Sarah Horne 2017

The moral rights of the author have been asserted

First published in this edition 2019

British Library Cataloguing in Publication Data
Data available

978-0-19-276910-7

1 3 5 7 9 10 8 6 4 2

Paper used in the production of this book is a natural, recyclable product
made from wood grown in sustainable forests. The manufacturing process
conforms to the environmental regulations of the country of origin.

Printed in China

Helping your child to read

Before they start

- Talk about the back cover blurb. How does your child think a chicken might get hold of lots of chocolate?

- Look at the front cover. Does your child think this is going to be a serious story or a funny one?

During reading

- Let your child read at their own pace, either silently or out loud.
- If necessary, help them to work out words they don't know by saying each sound out loud and then blending them to say the word, e.g. *g-r-ai-n, grain.*
- Encourage your child to keep checking that the text makes sense and they understand what they are reading. Remind them to re-read to check the meaning if they're not sure.
- Give them lots of praise for good reading!

After reading

- Look at page 48 for some fun activities.

Chapter One

Charlie was a chicken who liked chocolate.

She didn't like eating grain, or corn, or even dirt (yuk!).

No, Charlie liked chocolate.

But she didn't get it very often.

Charlie had only had a taste of
chocolate once, but she had remembered
it ever since.

Farmer Grice's little boy, Joe, had
come to pick up the eggs – while eating
a bar of chocolate. A tiny piece had
fallen on the floor.

When Joe had gone, Charlie pecked
up the tiny speck of chocolate and –
slowly – swallowed.

Her mind was
blown. It melted
in her mouth! It
was so sweet! Why
was she wasting
her time eating
grain when there were
delights like this?

"Well, that's it!" Charlie
announced to the rest of the chickens. "I'm
not eating grain any more! It's only –
only … *this stuff* for me."

She peered at the chocolate bar wrapper
which Joe had dropped. Unfortunately
Charlie couldn't read. (Most chickens
can't.)

The rest of the chickens looked up
for a second.

Then they carried on eating their grain.

Only Meg, Charlie's friend, came scurrying over.

"What is that?" she squawked. "Let me see, let me see!" Luckily for Charlie, Meg was one of the only chickens in the world who *could* read. She had found one of Joe's books on the grass one day (yes, Joe was a little careless) and studied it until the black marks started to make sense.

Milk chocolate

"Ch-o-c-o-l-a-t-e," spelled out Meg. "M-i-l-k chocolate. Oooh! Is it good?"

"Good?" said Charlie. "It's amazing!"

"Can I try a bit?" said Meg.

"Oh … er … sorry," said Charlie. "It's all gone." As indeed it had.

"Well, we need some more of this ch-o-c-o-l-a-t-e thing," said Charlie. "I won't eat any more grain until I get some, and I suggest you do the same."

Chapter Two

The next morning, Charlie and Meg sat in their coop with the chocolate bar wrapper laid out before them.

At feeding time, Farmer Grice came and dished out some grain for all the chickens. The rest of the chickens gobbled up the grain as if they hadn't eaten all week.

Charlie and Meg didn't touch their grain. Instead, they looked up at Farmer Grice appealingly with big, round eyes.

Farmer Grice was a busy man with a
fierce temper.

"Why are you two chickens looking
at me like that?" he growled.

Charlie did her best *"buck-buck-buuuuck,"* as if to say "Chocolate, please!" Meg nudged the wrapper forward with her beak.

"What's this thing here?" said Farmer Grice, picking up the wrapper. "Chocolate? You chickens want *chocolate?"*

Charlie and Meg jumped up and down. Feathers went everywhere.

"*Chocolate?* Chickens don't eat chocolate!" stormed Farmer Grice. "Chickens eat grain. That's all there is to it. And if you don't like it, you can eat nothing at all!"

He slammed the henhouse door.

There was silence in the coop.

The other hens looked at Charlie and Meg accusingly.

"Well, *I'm* only eating chocolate from now on!" said Charlie. "Come on, Meg, let's find Joe. He's sure to know where we can get some."

There was a little gap between the bottom of the henhouse and the ground. A small gap, but a gap nonetheless.

Charlie dived into it, feathers wobbling furiously. "Come on, Meg," she shouted. "Let's wriggle our way to choco-heaven!"

Meg looked at the crowd of dim chickens behind her. "Gotta go, girls," she said, "to somewhere far more egg-citing!"

Chapter Three

Charlie and Meg scuttled across the yard
to the Grices' house.

"Come on!" said Charlie. She climbed
in through the nearest window and
flopped inside, like a big, feathered ball.

Joe was
spreadeagled on
the floor, reading
a comic.

He jumped
up in surprise.
(Chickens didn't
fall in through
his window on a
daily basis.)

"Woah!" he said.
Meg tumbled over
the edge in a large
flurry of feathers.

"Another one," said Joe. "Even better! What are you two doing here?"

Charlie waddled over to Joe's comic. To her delight, she noticed an advertisement with a picture of a chocolate bar.

"*Buucck!*" she clucked, jumping up and down.

"Hey, get off my comic," said Joe.

Meg read the advert. "*Buck-buck-buuuck!*" she blurted, pointing her beak to each part of the word 'chocolate'.

Charlie stared at Joe with her little brown eyes. They suddenly reminded Joe of chocolate drops. She kept on staring.

"It's almost," Joe thought, "as if she wants something."

He edged nearer to Charlie and peered at the advert. "Not … chocolate?" He was almost submerged by the whirl of feathers.

"You want *chocolate*? Really? Well … I've none here, sorry. But hang on a minute, I know where there might be some … Come on!" He pointed to the door. "But you need to be quiet."

Chapter Four

Joe, Charlie and Meg crept into the kitchen.

There was a loud banging from outside. Mrs Grice was mending the tractor.

"We're looking for my mum's Secret Chocolate Box," whispered Joe. "Where is it?"

He looked in all the cupboards. "Better not let Mum see us."

BANG BANG BANG

Using their beaks, the two chickens started to open cupboards and drawers.

They found bowls, saucepans and cake tins.

They found flour, sugar and cocoa … but no chocolate.

Meg even found a recipe book. "Oooh, look," she said to Charlie. "Chocolate cake! Look, we've got everything we need here. Maybe—"

"Last one!" said Charlie, pouncing on a drawer. "It's a bit stiff …" The two chickens pulled on the drawer with all their might.

It sprang open – with a loud clattering of metal spoons.

CLANG!
BANG!

"Mum's going to hear!" hissed Joe.

The last ladle clattered on to the floor.

Joe and the chickens listened, nervously.

BONG!

Silence.

"Whew, that's OK," said Joe. "Now, let's try the fridge!" He reached in – "Yes!" – and brought out a plastic box, crammed with promising bars.

Charlie, however, was still listening, wide-eyed.

"Now it's *too* quiet!" she whispered to Meg.

She was right. The banging *outside* had stopped as well as the clattering *inside*.

Mrs Grice appeared in the doorway.

"WHAT IS GOING ON?" she yelled.

She seemed to have an entirely purple face.

Joe and the chickens looked up, guiltily.

"Er ... sorry, Mum," said Joe. "It's just that me – and, er, the chickens were hungry ..."

"Get out!" bellowed Mrs Grice. "How dare you go into my Secret Chocolate Box! And look at the state of this kitchen! Anyone would think we lived in a farmyard!"

She waved her wrench. Charlie, Joe and Meg scurried out of the kitchen as fast as their legs would carry them.

Chapter Five

Luckily, Meg spotted the village shop
at the end of the lane. She did her best
squawking and flapping act to show
Joe what he needed to do next.

"Of course!" said Joe, beaming. "I've
got some pocket money. Let's go!"

They set off for Mrs Pumpernickel's
Village Shop.

Mrs Pumpernickel kept her shop obsessively tidy, despite owning a shop very close to a muddy farm. Joe thought she would not appreciate having Charlie and Meg going through her chocolate display.

So, one feather-filled minute later, Joe strode into Mrs Pumpernickel's shop with two chickens stuffed up his jumper.

"Hello, Joe," said Mrs Pumpernickel. "Has your mum run out of nails? Or has your dad run out of chicken feed?"

At the mention of chicken feed, Meg tried to make a run for it.

Charlie grabbed her. "Don't do it!" she hissed.

"You all right, Joe?" said Mrs Pumpernickel.

"Yes, thank you Mrs P, I'm fine," stammered Joe. "I'd, er, just like a bar of chocolate."

But the smell of chocolate was too much for Charlie. She flew out from underneath Joe's jumper. Meg swiftly followed.

"Chickens?" shrieked Mrs Pumpernickel. "I can't have chickens in my shop!"

"Sorry, Mrs Pumpernickel," said Joe, chasing after them.

"It's not allowed! It's not permitted!
It's against Health and Safety Shop
Regulations!" yelled Mrs Pumpernickel.

Charlie and Meg were like chickens
in a sweet shop.

"Look!" said Charlie. "There's
chocolate everywhere, Meg!"

Mrs Pumpernickel, meanwhile, had fetched a large broom. "I have *one* rule," she said, "and that is: no chickens in this shop!"

And with that, she booted all three of them out of the door, and left them there, in a cloud of dust.

"That went well," said Charlie.

"Hang on a minute," said Joe, thinking hard. "It's my school trip tomorrow ... and we're going to ... the chocolate factory!"

Chapter Six

It had been a long night, and a long journey. Charlie and Meg had spent the night under Joe's bed. Now they were peeping out from the top of his rucksack on the school coach.

"Callaway's Chocolate Factory," read Meg.

Charlie sniffed the air delightedly. "We're here, Meg," she squawked. "Chocolate for lunch!"

"Now hold on, you chickens," whispered Joe. "I'm not allowed to bring fizzy drinks on this trip, never mind *two chickens*. You have to stay in *here*." He gently pushed them back in the bag. Then, following the rest of his class, he walked in, rucksack on his back, through the factory gates.

As soon as he could, Joe let the chickens out of the bag. The factory

was not as exciting as they had
expected. There were lots of pictures
of beans, sunshine and sugar. But
no chocolate.

"This is boring," Charlie said.

Meg, however, was reading all
the labels. "This is amazing!" she said.
"Did you know that—"

"No!" said Charlie. "I don't care
how it's made! I just want to eat it!"

Her clucking was louder than she'd intended. Joe's teacher looked around as Joe stuffed the chickens back into his rucksack. "Did you say something, Joe?" she said.

"Er, no, Miss Western," said Joe. "I was just, er, wondering when we're having lunch."

"Soon," said the teacher. "We've got a treat first – we're going to see a cooking demonstration by Egbert E."

"Who's Egbert E?" said Joe, along with the rest of the class.

"Egbert E," said the teacher, "is a famous chef. You are *very* lucky to see him!"

"I want some chocolate," said one child.

"I'd like some lunch," said another.

Joe sat down with the rest of his class, all with grumbles in their heads and their tummies.

"Here is …" boomed a voice, "EGBERT E!"

A spindly man in a white suit walked
out on to the stage. He had a short,
orange haircut and very large glasses.
He didn't smile.

"Hello," he said.

There was silence from the
unimpressed, hungry audience.

Which included, of course,
two chickens.

Chapter Seven

Egbert E didn't look too pleased to
be there.

"I suppose you want to see some
baking, do you?" he sighed. "Boring.
Honestly, if I have to make another
cake …"

He carried on muttering and
complaining as he brought out the
ingredients: flour, sugar, butter and …
five enormous slabs of chocolate, the
size of dinner plates.

Tantalizing whiffs of chocolate
wafted around the audience.

"I will tell you one thing, if I have to," sniffed Egbert. "*Fresh* ingredients are key to baking. That's all I have to say."

Then he smashed the chocolate into tiny pieces with a rolling pin.

Inside the rucksack, Charlie's mouth was watering. "I'm going to have some of that chocolate," she said.

"Charlie," hissed Meg. "Come back!"

But Charlie was already out of the bag and waddling over to the stage.

Egbert E was now melting the chocolate, which made the delicious smell even more intense.

No one noticed as Charlie hopped up on to the stage.

Egbert E's head disappeared under the counter, looking for something. "Where are the eggs? How can I bake without eggs?" He was getting quite cross.

Charlie flapped up on to the table. Egbert E still had his head stuck underneath. "This is *unacceptable!*" he said. Now he sounded furious.

"Look!" shouted the children in the audience. Egbert E lifted his head – and came face-to-face with Charlie.

"Good grief," he said.

Charlie looked at Egbert, at the audience, and at the chocolate.

She was so excited, she didn't quite know what to do with herself.

So she laid an egg.

Chapter Eight

In the audience, Joe was trembling.

"Oh no," he said. "We're done for now."
To his horror, Meg was now waddling
up to join her friend.

Big, burly chocolate factory men
came rushing up the aisle. "Sorry, sir,"
said one of the men to Egbert E. "We'll
soon have this sorted out." He tried to
catch the flapping birds – but failed.

The audience held its breath.

But Egbert was looking delightedly at the egg that Charlie had laid. "That," he said, "is what I call a *fresh* ingredient! Do you have any more?" Meg, joining Charlie, was only too happy to oblige. Within a minute, there was another large, warm, brown egg on the counter.

"Fabulastic!" shouted Egbert E. "Would you mind, ladies?"

"Of course not," said Charlie (which, naturally, sounded like "*Buck buck buckkk,*" to the audience).

Egbert broke one of the eggs into the bowl. "A double-yolker!" he yelled. "This is tremendous!"

"Now," said Egbert, adding in the melted chocolate, "we just need …"

Meg, who had been studying the recipe on the table, nudged over a big bag labelled 'flour'.

"I don't believe it! A chicken that can read!" said Egbert.

Charlie brought over the baking tins while Egbert stirred in the flour. Then she brought over a spatula to help get the mixture out of the bowl.

The audience loved it.

"This is much quicker than normal!" said Egbert E. "And much more fun, too! How can I thank you glorious girls?" There were a few crumbs of chocolate left on the table. Charlie looked longingly at them. "You ... want some chocolate? Go ahead!"

Charlie pecked up some chocolate. It was delightful. It was delectable. It was delicious! "Try some, Meg," she called.

Meg tried some, and nearly swooned. "You were right, Charlie," she said, "this is *amazing*!"

To everyone's delight, the chickens clucked together in close harmony. Egbert E threw out a hand. "Ladies and gentlemen, I present to you my new assistants – the chicken chefs!"

In the audience, Joe clapped until his hands nearly came off, as Charlie and Meg proudly bowed.

CLAP CLAP CLAP!

Chapter Nine

Life was never the same again for
Charlie or Meg. Or Joe, come to that.
Egbert E quickly realized that these
chickens had star quality, and invited
them to join his new 'Egg-stra-ordinary'
cooking tour.

Meg read the recipes and Charlie
brought out the right bowls, spoons and
whisks. They laid eggs on cue. They
clucked, they flapped, they waddled,
they pecked.

Soon, Egbert and his egg-stra-special guests had their own TV show and had written a new recipe book.

Joe came along with them, to look after them.

Farmer Grice provided them with chicken feed. (The Grices' farm went from strength to strength now it was known as the Chicken Chef Farm.) For Charlie had started to eat grain again. She'd realized that – maybe – she couldn't live on chocolate alone.

But she could have a treat now and then.

And so, as payment for their work, Meg and Charlie – and Joe – got a piece of chocolate every single day.

After reading activities

Quick quiz

See how fast you can answer these questions!
Look back at the story if you can't remember.

1 How does Charlie get her first taste of chocolate?

2 How does Charlie tell Joe that she wants more chocolate?

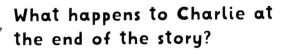

3 What happens to Charlie at the end of the story?

Try this!

What do you think is the funniest part of the story? Draw a picture of it, and add a speech bubble.

1) Joe drops some and she pecks it up; 2) she uses her beak to point at the word 'chocolate' in an advert; 3) she becomes a famous cookery star